Learn With Animals

In the Forest

By Laura Ottina
Adapted by Barbara Bakowski

Illustrated by
Sebastiano Ranchetti

WEEKLY READER®
PUBLISHING

From high in the trees
To deep underground,
In the green forest
Is where we are found.

3

4

I am a green woodpecker,
With a red feathered cap
And a long, pointy bill
That goes tap, tap, tap.

I am a squirrel,
With a tail that is furry.
Among the tree branches
I jump and I scurry.

7

8

I am a red fox
With a thick, fluffy coat,
Golden eyes, pointy ears,
And white fur on my throat.

I am a badger
With a face black and white.
To hunt I come out
Of my burrow at night.

I am a red deer.

I grow new antlers each year.

I shed them in winter,

And in spring they appear!

I am a boar,
A kind of wild pig.
I have a strong snout
And teeth so big!

16

I am a wise owl
With big eyes and good sight.
They help me hunt food
In the forest at night.

I am a polecat,
Brown and small-sized.
I spray a bad smell
When I am surprised!

19

I am a brown bear.
In the winter I'm found
In a big, cozy den,
Where I sleep safe and sound.

I am a hedgehog,
As cute as a bug,
But my back has sharp spines
So don't give me a hug!

23

Please visit our web site at **www.garethstevens.com**.
For a free catalog describing our list of high-quality books,
call 1-800-542-2595 (USA) or 1-800-387-3178 (Canada).
Our fax: 1-877-542-2596

Library of Congress Cataloging-in-Publication Data
Ottina, Laura.
   [Incontra gli animali nella foresta. English]
   In the forest / by Laura Ottina ; adapted by Barbara Bakowski ;
illustrated by Sebastiano Ranchetti.
      p. cm. – (Learn with animals)
   ISBN-10: 1-4339-1912-5   ISBN-13: 978-1-4339-1912-1 (lib. bdg.)
   ISBN-10: 1-4339-2089-1   ISBN-13: 978-1-4339-2089-9 (softcover)
   1. Forest animals–Juvenile literature. I. Bakowski, Barbara. II. Ranchetti, Sebastiano, ill.
III. Title.
QL112.08813   2010
591.73–dc22
                                           2008052369

This North American edition first published in 2010 by
Weekly Reader® Books
An Imprint of Gareth Stevens Publishing
1 Reader's Digest Road
Pleasantville, NY 10570-7000 USA

This U.S. edition copyright © 2010 by Gareth Stevens, Inc. International Copyright © 2008 by
Editoriale Jaca Book spa, Milan, Italy. All rights reserved. First published in 2008 as
Incontra gli animali nella foresta by Editoriale Jaca Book spa.

Gareth Stevens Executive Managing Editor: Lisa M. Herrington
Gareth Stevens Senior Editor: Barbara Bakowski
Gareth Stevens Creative Director: Lisa Donovan
Gareth Stevens Designer: Jennifer Ryder-Talbot

Printed in the United States of America

1 2 3 4 5 6 7 8 9 12 11 10 09

Find out more about Laura Ottina and Sebastiano Ranchetti at **www.animalsincolor.com**.